Amazing Animals

Critter Camp

Division

Linda Ruggieri, M.A.T.

Contributing Author
Kat Bernardo, M.Ed.

Consultants
Michele Ogden, Ed.D
Principal, Irvine Unified School District

Jennifer Robertson, M.A.Ed.
Teacher, Huntington Beach City School District

Publishing Credits
Rachelle Cracchiolo, M.S.Ed., *Publisher*
Conni Medina, M.A.Ed., *Managing Editor*
Dona Herweck Rice, *Series Developer*
Emily R. Smith, M.A.Ed., *Series Developer*
Diana Kenney, M.A.Ed., NBCT, *Content Director*
Stacy Monsman, M.A., *Editor*
Kevin Panter, *Graphic Designer*

Image Credits: p. 4 Image Source/Getty Images; p. 7 dpa picture alliance/Alamy Stock Photo; p. 8 The Science Picture Company/Alamy Stock Photo; p. 9 Picture by Tambako the Jaguar/Getty Images; p. 15 John Cancalosi/Getty Images; p. 16 Wild Horizons/UIG via Getty Images; pp. 18–19 PhotoStock-Israel/Alamy Stock Photo; p. 20 (top) NOAA/Alamy Stock Photo, (middle) Joel Sartore/Getty Images, (bottom) US Coast Guard Photo/Alamy Stock Photo; p. 21 Felix Choo/Alamy Stock Photo; all other images from iStock and/or Shutterstock.

Teacher Created Materials
5301 Oceanus Drive
Huntington Beach, CA 92649-1030
http://www.tcmpub.com

ISBN 978-1-4807-5800-1
© 2018 Teacher Created Materials, Inc.
Made in China
Nordica.022017.CA21700227

Table of Contents

Welcome to Critter Camp! 4

Day 1: Just Call Me Dr. Callie! 6

Day 2: Time to Play! 10

Day 3: Build a Habitat Challenge 14

Day 4: Protection Patrol 18

Day 5: Animal Fact Showdown 22

Good-Bye, Campers! 26

Problem Solving 28

Glossary 30

Index 31

Answer Key 32

Welcome to Critter Camp!

Each summer, over one hundred million visitors walk through the gates of zoos. They spend the day watching animals. Some go to see a certain **exhibit**. They might even take a few pictures. At the end of the day, they head home, happy about what they saw.

But Rose, Ben, Javi, and Callie want to do more than just look at animals. They want to be junior zookeepers for a week at their local zoo. So, they are going to a special summer camp. This will be no mere stroll around the zoo. They will get to see things that other visitors can only dream of seeing. During their week at camp, they will help build **habitats**. They will help sick animals. The campers will learn how to guard **endangered** animals, too. Join them as they head off to Critter Camp!

Rose, Ben, Javi, and Callie

Day 1: Just Call Me Dr. Callie!

Today was my first day at Critter Camp, and it was awesome! First, I met my group leader, Counselor Chip. Then, I met the other campers. Their names are Rose, Ben, and Javi. Next, Chip gave us our assignments for the day. I got to visit Dr. Carter at the zoo's animal hospital. Chip said Dr. Carter needed help taking care of a wolf pup.

The wolf pup was in rough shape. Yesterday, he was playing with his pack. But today, he just wanted to sleep. Dr. Carter was worried that he might have a virus. This would explain why he seemed so tired. Dr. Carter let me help while she held the wolf pup. The poor pup looked so scared! So, I stroked his soft fur to keep him calm. Dr. Carter drew a sample of the wolf's blood. The pup was so brave! He didn't yelp at all. I like to think I had something to do with that.

wolf pack

A wildlife park worker holds a wolf pup while it gets a vaccination.

mother and cub

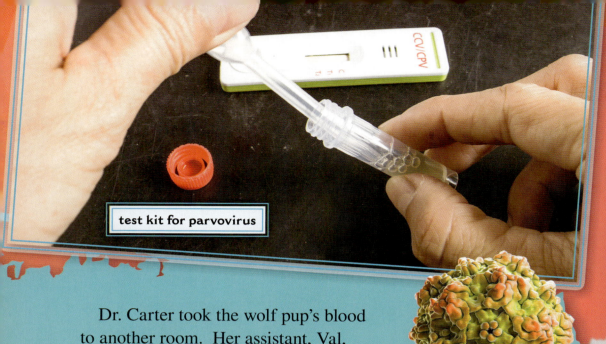

test kit for parvovirus

close-up of parvovirus particles

Dr. Carter took the wolf pup's blood to another room. Her assistant, Val, would see if the blood contained **parvovirus** (PAR-vo-vi-rus). Meanwhile, Dr. Carter let me watch as she checked the wolf pup's teeth. She slowly opened the pup's mouth and looked inside. He had a lot of teeth, but some were missing. Dr. Carter said that wolves are born with baby teeth just like us. She called them *milk teeth*. This pup had lost some of his milk teeth, and he had some permanent teeth growing.

Val came back with the results. The wolf pup tested positive for parvovirus. Dr. Carter told us not to worry, though. The pup would spend a few days in the zoo's clinic. He would have to take medicine, but he would be as good as new in about a week!

I wanted to bring the wolf pup back to my bunk. But, Val reminded me that he is a wild animal. No matter how cute a wild animal may be, you should never touch it without a trained adult nearby.

milk teeth

permanent teeth

LET'S EXPLORE MATH

Dr. Carter tells Callie that by the time a wolf pup is about 28 weeks old, all of its milk teeth have been replaced by permanent teeth. About how many months old is a wolf pup when it has all of its permanent teeth?

Day 2: Time to Play!

Today, we learned about something called **enrichment**. Things like books, toys, bikes, games, and activities keep our minds active. Animals need to keep their minds busy, too. This helps them learn and keeps them happy.

Today, Counselor Chip asked us to observe elephants in their **enclosure**. Then, he asked us to create enrichment items for them. The items would help keep their minds active. Counselor Chip wanted the elephants to see, smell, hear, taste, or touch something in the activity. This was going to be hard. So, Ben and I decided to work together.

First, we headed to the elephant habitat. We wanted to see how they played together. We saw one elephant use her trunk to suck up water. Then, she sprayed it on herself. Ben thought this helped her cool down. We also noticed elephants wrestling with their friends. They really liked rolling in the mud!

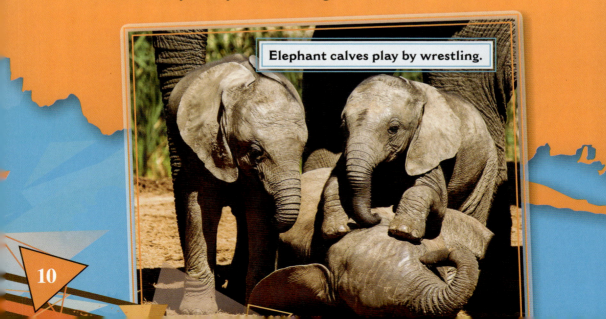

Elephant calves play by wrestling.

An elephant sprays water on itself.

Next, Ben and I read the signs around the exhibit. We learned that elephants can eat up to 600 pounds (275 kilograms) of food each day. They spend almost 20 hours per day eating!

This gave us an idea for our enrichment activity. We could use food as part of a game. We asked the counselors for help finding materials. They gave us some barrels. We filled the barrels with hay, carrots, and lettuce. We put the tops on tight. That way, the elephants would have to figure out how to get the food.

Elephants play with tires as part of an enrichment program.

We wanted the elephants to use their sense of smell, too. Since they eat so much, we decided to use more food. We grabbed bananas, grapes, and apples. Then, we put the food into tires. Ben and I wrapped rope around each tire to keep the food inside. Then, we asked Counselor Chip to hide the tires around the elephants' habitat.

Adult elephants can eat up to 2,000 bananas a day!

LET'S EXPLORE MATH

1. Callie and Ben have 5 barrels and 100 pounds of hay. How much hay can go into each barrel?
2. There are 36 bananas. Callie and Ben want to put 6 bananas in each tire. How many tires can they fill for the elephants?

Day 3: Build a Habitat Challenge

After breakfast today, we got to visit the panda exhibit. Counselor Chip asked us to describe what we saw. I pointed out a grassy field with a large cave in the middle of the exhibit. Javi noticed a pool and a stream. Rose spotted bamboo growing against a fence. Counselor Chip said we found all the **elements** of a habitat. Every creature needs space, shelter, water, and food.

A panda rests in its habitat.

horned lizard

a horned lizard after it has squirted blood out of its eye

After lunch, Counselor Chip walked us to the reptile building. He explained that our next challenge was to build a new habitat for the reptiles. First, we had to pick a reptile. Then, we had to research the type of habitat it needs. Finally, we had to build the habitat.

The best part was that we got to put real reptiles in our habitats! I chose a horned lizard. My little brother loves them because they can squirt blood from their eyes! They do it for protection from wolves, dogs, and coyotes. The squirting confuses them. Also, the blood can be harmful to those animals. But I still think it is gross!

I knew I needed to give the horned lizard plenty of space. I read that it should have an enclosure that is three times its length. Since the horned lizard was about 5 inches (13 centimeters) long, I knew it would need a 15-inch (38-cm) tank. I decided to put sand, sticks, and dry leaves at the bottom of the tank. Horned lizards live in warm climates, so I added a heat lamp. Next, I grabbed some rocks and built a little cave. All that was still needed was the food. Ants are on the menu! I gently poured a few ants into the tank and shut the lid tightly.

Counselor Chip brought over a horned lizard from the reptile room. He carefully opened the tank and placed the lizard on the sand. At first, the lizard stood very still. Then, it spotted an ant and quickly grabbed it with its tongue. The lizard started to explore its new home. I think he liked it!

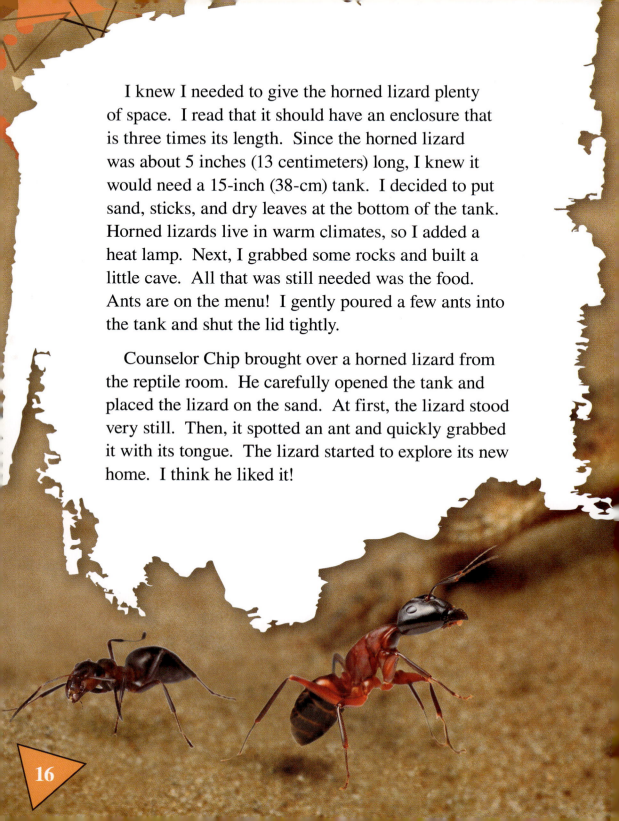

horned lizard

LET'S EXPLORE MATH

1. The zoo gets ants in containers of 1,000. An adult horned lizard can eat about 100 ants per day. How many days will a container of ants last?

2. Callie feeds the horned lizard 5 ants at a time. If the lizard eats 100 ants, how many feedings will the horned lizard need?

Day 4: Protection Patrol

Counselor Chip woke us up really early today. He said we were going on a trip! We packed our bags and went to the van. Once Counselor Chip got in the van, he told us all about sea turtles. He said they are endangered because of hunting, fishing, and **pollution**. He said we would spend the day helping to clean some baby sea turtles that got stuck in an oil spill.

We arrived at the Sea Turtle **Rehabilitation** Center, where we met Dr. North. She told us that pollution is one of the biggest **threats** to sea turtles. Sea turtles might eat dirty food or get stuck in garbage. They can also breathe oil into their lungs.

Turtles move around a lot during their lives. So, pollution can threaten them wherever they go. A sea turtle's life starts on land. The mother digs a hole and lays her eggs. When the eggs hatch, **hatchlings** crawl out. Then, they head for the ocean. They might come into contact with pollution in any of those places!

A sea turtle lays eggs on the beach.

sea turtle eggs and a hatchling in the sand

A hatchling moves away from oil.

Dr. North brought us into the lab, where she showed us a large pool filled with hatchlings. She explained that they arrived yesterday. They were tired, cold, and scared. Her team placed the turtles under heat lamps so they could warm up. After a good night's sleep, they were ready to be cleaned!

A veterinarian gets ready to clean oil off a sea turtle in the Gulf of Mexico.

clean hatchlings

The turtles were very **dehydrated**. Dr. North showed me how to use a **syringe** to give them small amounts of water. Then, she brought out a jar of mayonnaise. I thought it was time for lunch, but Dr. North said we were going to use it to clean the turtles! She explained that the mayonnaise mixes with the oil. The mixture can then be wiped off with a towel. Once we wiped them off, we gave the hatchlings a quick scrub with soap and warm water. Finally, we dried them with very soft towels. The turtles seemed much happier now that they were clean and warm.

LET'S EXPLORE MATH

The campers are going to wash 20 turtles. They use one cup of mayonnaise to wash each turtle. One jar of mayonnaise has 4 cups in it. How many jars of mayonnaise will they need?

A hatchling falls asleep in a rescue worker's hand.

mayonnaise

Day 5: Animal Fact Showdown

Today was the day I was waiting for all week. It was the Animal Fact Showdown! In Round One, we had to choose which animal we thought was the strongest.

Rose and I chose an African elephant. We remembered reading that elephants can carry over 19,000 lbs. (8,600 kg) on their backs. Ben chose tigers, which he read can carry 1,200 lbs. (550 kg). Javi chose…dung beetles. We all laughed. Dung beetles are so small! They can only pull 50 lbs. (23 kg)! I was ready to win the first round.

dung beetle

But, Javi stopped me. He said that since dung beetles are so small, 50 lbs. is actually amazing. That is over 1,000 times their body weight! Ben, Rose, and I went back to our books. Tigers can carry two times their body weight. And elephants can only carry a little over one time their own body weight. It looks like Javi was right after all!

LET'S EXPLORE MATH

1. The campers know that a tiger can carry two times its body weight. If a male tiger carries 220 kilograms, how much does it weigh?

2. A female tiger at the zoo weighs about 70 kilograms. How many kilograms can it carry?

Javi was happy that he won the first round, but I had a good feeling about the next one! In Round Two, we had to choose which animal we thought was the fastest. I was sure cheetahs would win. Javi chose peregrine falcons. Rose picked brown hares. Ben agreed with Rose.

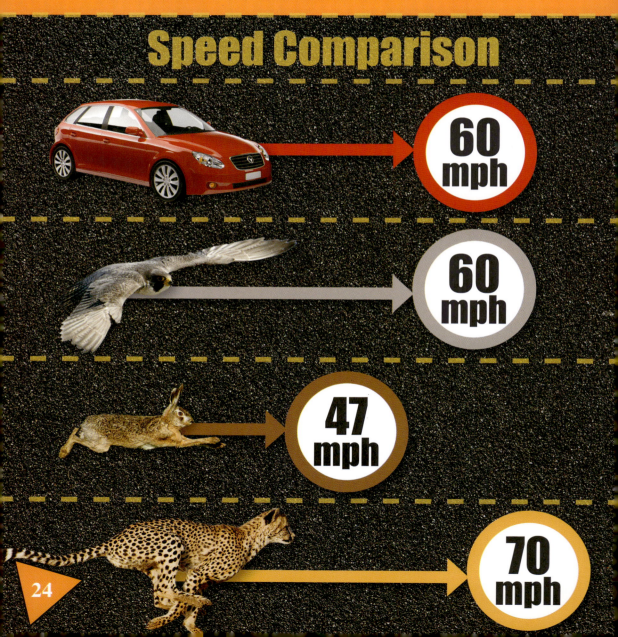

Again, we hit the books, looking for facts. Ben was the first to find a fact this time. He said that brown hares can run about 47 miles (75 kilometers) per hour. That is fast, but not fast enough to win this competition! I found that cheetahs can run up to 70 mph (110 kmph). That is faster than a car driving on a highway! Javi found some information about peregrine falcons. He said that they can fly up to 60 mph (100 kmph). I thought for sure it was my turn to win. But, no such luck! When falcons dive, they can reach speeds of 240 mph (390 kmph). Javi won again!

peregrine falcon

LET'S EXPLORE MATH

The campers found that peregrine falcons can dive at speeds up to 240 miles per hour.

1. If a peregrine falcon is flying at 40 miles per hour, how many times faster can it dive?

2. If a peregrine falcon is flying at 60 miles per hour, how many times faster can it dive?

Good-Bye, Campers!

The Animal Fact Showdown marked the end of Critter Camp. I had to say goodbye to all of my new friends. I went to the animal hospital to check on the wolf pup. He was feeling much better and was playing with his pack again. Dr. Carter said he made a full **recovery**.

Next, I strolled over to the elephants. It was so exciting to see that they were still playing with the toys we made! They had not figured out how to open the food-filled barrel yet, but they were getting close. After that, I stopped by the reptile house to see whether the horned lizard still liked its habitat. Sure enough, it was warming itself under the heat lamp.

Then, it was time to say good-bye to Ben, Rose, Javi, and Counselor Chip. We all promised that we would keep helping animals. I am already looking forward to seeing them again next year at Critter Camp!

Problem Solving

Dung beetles do something most people consider gross. Dung beetles drink the liquid found in dung (poop!). They lay their eggs on dung balls. They also bury dung. All of their hard work helps to improve soil. It also helps to keep fly populations under control.

They are so good at waste disposal that they were brought to Australia to help with a problem. There weren't enough dung beetles in the country to handle all of the solid waste, or **cowpats**. So, dung beetles were brought to the country's cattle pastures to bury the dung. Solve the problems to find out more about dung beetles.

1. One cow can produce about 84 cowpats each week. How many cowpats is this per day?

2. Without dung beetles, one cowpat can become home to 3,000 flies in two weeks! How many flies is this per week?

3. A female dung beetle can lay up to 20 eggs at a time. But, she might not lay them all on one dung ball. If a female lays the same number of eggs on each dung ball, what are all the possible ways this could be done?

cowpat

Glossary

cowpats—pieces of solid waste that come from cows

dehydrated—lost too much water

elements—specific parts

enclosure—a space that is closed in by a wall or fence

endangered—used to describe an animal or plant that is at risk of completely dying out

enrichment—the process of increasing the quality of something

exhibit—an object or space that has been put out for people to look at

habitats—the places where plants and animals usually live or grow

hatchlings—very young animals that have just come out of eggs

parvovirus—a disease that causes loss of appetite, vomiting, and lethargy

pollution—the act of making land, water, or air dirty and unsafe

recovery—the process of becoming healthy again after an injury or illness

rehabilitation—a treatment that brings someone or something back to health

syringe—a device that is used to put fluids into or take them out of the body

threats—things that can cause trouble or harm

Index

ants, 16–17

brown hares, 24–25

cheetahs, 24–25

dung beetle, 22–23, 28–29

elephants, 10, 12–13, 22–23, 26

enrichment, 10, 12

habitat, 4, 10, 13–15, 26

hatchlings, 18, 20–21

horned lizard, 15–17, 26

milk teeth, 8–9

panda, 14

parvovirus, 8

peregrine falcon, 24–25

reptile, 15–16, 26

sea turtles, 19, 26

tiger, 22–23

wolf, 6–8, 26

Answer Key

Let's Explore Math

page 9:
7 months

page 13:
1. 20 pounds
2. 6 tires

page 17:
1. 10 days
2. 20 feedings

page 21:
5 jars

page 23:
1. 110 kg
2. 140 kg

page 25:
1. 6 times faster
2. 4 times faster

Problem Solving

1. 12 cowpats per day
2. 1,500 flies per week
3. 1 dung ball, 20 eggs;
   2 dung balls, 10 eggs each;
   4 dung balls, 5 eggs each;
   5 dung balls, 4 eggs each;
   10 dung balls, 2 eggs each;
   20 dung balls, 1 egg each